FREEDOM IS

Ask me about
Hope
Pain
Street Drama
We are
emotional scars with trauma

Outdated neighborhoods
being some good
wish I can stop being
misunderstood
be better but never
forever

Defeating oppressors
mailing protest letters
finding ancestors
raising legacies
nothing will stop me
as far as the eye can see

Wanting safer schools
Educating with more tools
Clean drinking water
Help mental disorders
Heal for the Homeless
Real progress

Their whole program
is out of pocket
Stick paper clips in
The light sockets
No one profits
so why are we compliant?

No more colored prisons
right decisions
Same page or same mission
indifference has no
permission
or conversation

Piss free sidewalks
lying Politicians don't talk
no more lines of chalk
Trash doesn't exist in allies and real affordable housing
Life is a new outing
So is the money no one is counting

Jim Crow created Ghettos
producing negative embryos
positive died some years ago
I speak for the unspoken
often misused as tokens
all those spirits broken

Seasons have meaning
love stop reasoning
hate isn't disappearing
we need unrestricted access
souls willing to confess
psyche seems to be depressed

My first book will enlighten
My audience will inspire as my deliver will transpire
This one word we all deserve
With new pronouns and verbs
Tired of being robbed as I'm concerned
so is Freedom

FREEDOM

VAGABOND
VENICE/CULVER CITY, CA

FREEDOM

WOODROW BAILEY

VAGABOND

Copyright © 2022 Woodrow Bailey
Edition Copyright © 2022 Mark Lipman, editor
Front Cover Artwork: From the Conscious Series- Concept 1
Copyright © 2022 Woodrow Bailey
Back Cover Photography: Copyright © 2022 Full Image 360
All rights reserved.

No part of this book may be reproduced by any means, including information storage and retrieval or photocopying, except for short excerpts quoted in critical articles, without the written permission of the publisher.

editor@vagabondbooks.net

Published by VAGABOND
Mark Lipman, editor

Intellectual Property
Bailey, Woodrow
Freedom
1st ed. / p.cm.

ISBN13: 978-1-958307-00-7
Made in the USA.

ACKNOWLEDGEMENTS

The old saying goes "It's been a long time coming." Now it's here as we are our own worst critic. If we are true to ourselves, we can do whatever we set our minds to. I remember an Artist making a statement saying he was a thirty-year overnight sensation, I was a young and naïve to the hard work, dedication and effort it took be successful creatively. That success is left up to the reader to decide in reading this work.

My village has been a part of who I am and without them I do not accomplish any of this or have the quality of life I have. It's been a true blessing which goes beyond measure for each one of the them are a building block to my foundation.

God

My Wife and Children (Tahnda, Skylarr & Spencer)

My Mother (Gladys) for strength and perseverance

My Pop (Woodrow) the original WoodnHood

My Siblings (Christine, Maxine & Eric) we made it

My Sister (Stephanie) thank you

My Grandparents (Henry & Annie Bell Bailey, Alberta Foggan & James Robinson) for surviving the Great Depression, World War II & the Jim Crow South

Future books will reveal more of my village.

Special Thanks: To the Community Literature Initiative, the first step was the hardest but your guidance was instrumental.

#CLITuesdayClass8

To All Who Know Me...Peace & Faith

For all who know me, Bailey Woods is the creative spectrum of me. The creative alter ego of Woodrow Bailey.

It's all good Woods
go some more Drow
the pen name is
an alter ego
creating prose
story goes
Pen to Page Rage
has a soul
and a goal

TABLE OF CONTENTS

Foreword	10
Gave Genesis	15-27
Exit Exodus	29-44
Those Numbers	45-65
Neighborhood-logy	67-81
Observe My Revelation	83-93
Freedom Songs	95-108
Freedom's Freedom	109-120
Tributes & Pleas	121-132
See Me	133-140

FOREWORD

Woodrow Bailey: "Freedom"
"To write is to produce meaning and reproduce a pre-existing meaning ... poetry is never about something it is something".
Poetics and Precarity Myung Mi Kim and Cristanne Miller, Introduction pxiii, 2018

"There were no black images of dignity, no images of beautiful black people. There was this black hole I tried to fill." Roy DeCarava
"Roy Dearava Obituary," by Richard Williams,
www.The Guardian.com – Nov. 6, 2009

Photography and now poetry informs Woodrow Bailey's way of looking at the world. I still embrace my former USC student Woodrow Bailey's photographic mode almost 35 years ago...At that time his photographs described empathically, his daily encounters with his immediate present and his community. Collectively his images began a narrative that both defined and transcended boundaries.

In photography and in poetry Woodrow Bailey shapes the weight of moments collapsed beyond their kin with an urgent poetic journey burned into our nation's present. Woodrow's words cry their meanings as both a private and public condition. He summarizes the personal as he lays bare the shared.

Robert Flick
Professor Emeritus
Roski School of Art & Design
University of Southern California

I can tell you the definition of the word "Freedom" but what good will it do for your psyche? The condition of being free, are we? Think about this, we are being held hostage by others' drama, check the news or social media. Political independence, really, have you seen the latest parade of "Politicians" running for office. The mere word "Freedom" came with a cost, but no one wants to pay anymore.

Sure, you can move around this country with virtually no barriers but the psychological warfare in the minds of those who struggle is a real issue. We are not unrestricted by any means then again what do we have access to? I have a bird eye view of these conditions in my everyday environment. In fact, you see it too. I am recording it with the rage of my pen and paper.

Think about your freedom, your history and your ancestors, if you had to buy your freedom then what?

These phases are unique
discrete
they seek to
extract thoughts or
inject hope
cope
with Track 1
with a different sun
burning with
my journey
documentation
presentation
visualization
expressed
gives you verbal access

Postscript:

This is my own style and if you read any of my other material there are still a few surprises. Talk to you at the end. My village of family, friends, who have encouraged me to express who I am and as always this is for all who know me.

FREEDOM

GAVE GENESIS 1-10

FREEDOM 1

Claustrophobic trapped and tired of
Being held hostage by others drama
As they fill suitcases of destruction destroying the

Guilty and Innocent
Family and Friends
Lovers and Haters

In their subconscious, it's a right
We are privilege to witness this chaos
Surrounded by all methods of media

Begging for some measure of reform
As our tax dollars suffer scorn aiding and abiding
Socio-economical criminals seeking an addendum through

Public Assistance
Incarceration
Homelessness

Needing to administer mental health
Adhering to nothing and admired for everything
The previous prose asks the same questions

Street Drama
Pain
Hope

Accommodating no answers
The weight of inertia
As we all suffer in frustration

Adversary
Angry
Avenging

What way is this to operate?

Freedom

FREEDOM 2

Catastrophic
What was her mindset seeing in him?
Love in these neighborhoods is a trifling hustler

Some think of you as convenient
Others say you're transparent
More want you to be omniscient

Sporadically, you never said any of these adjectives
Not subjective then what's the objective?
Righteousness, resurrection and reflection

When is the manhunt? Only knowing a tiny slice of the universe
The result to apprehend so to attain so why is that music in your head?
Threatening with his mental health which was sleeping with domestic
violence

By product: Baby murdered
Side moment: Momma lifeless
Circumstance: horrific

Now what can she say? Where could she go?
We couldn't know, they shouldn't show and I wouldn't grow
As a concerned citizen but it's anticlimactic
Booked into the system with pretense, premeditated mission
Induced by a controlled substance (crystal met)
Street name with common sense all our attitudes are dense

How can I or any of us still believe in you?

Freedom

FREEDOM 3

Catatonic
Tears of anger burn my eyes as many others
Now sanctuaries of faith are war zones
Killing fields with all the previous prose can stand up
Claiming to cleanse his race and deface the presence of
Innocent Black (African American) lives that matter

Another lost soul decided to play God
What god does he serve?
Why would decide to stop dreams?
How did he determine his course?
When did this moment of psychosis started?
Who can save any of us?

Our young black men are being persecuted
Our young black women are treated like objects
Our black seniors are thrown away as trash

A flag that represents all this hate still flies and cries so take it down
Those who still believe all is well in America walk into an urban area
The South that's not your right so pray
The yesterdays, todays and tomorrows you think will happen
As tragedies are supposed to galvanize the collective
Will accountability or responsibility but not Democracy or any
Confederacy

Where a civil war can make love to maniac's mind breeding
Domestic Terrorism ignored yet we are held hostage by injustice
Prejudice
Malice
Bigotry
Terror

The soldering truth can't be put out or smoked
Keep thinking this is not at your doorstep
Our ancestors fought without any regrets
Freedom

FREEDOM 4

Just cause for the just or unjust pause
The maturity with senselessness of Jim Crow
He's still attacking our women now as they

Pronounce
Denounce
Announce

Another senseless death under suspicious circumstances

Suicide
Genocide
Homicide

Above the haze of horror that consumes her psyche in

Fear
Near
Unclear

Burning on the back burner of outrage
Another serving of anger so we're full and sick of it
Ancestors cry out from their lynching trees
Undeserved fire continues to roast their souls
She begs to return to settle the score nevertheless
Her family grieves receiving lie after lie as if they were leftovers

Unusual
Unsatisfying
Useless

Her future handcuffed actually shackled
The color of authority against the specter of sympathy
Can anyone be specific? Sadly this can happen to you

Her defiance with compliance becomes reliance of fair and impartial
treatment
Counterbalances resonate with the history of us
How many decades will this go unsolved?

Freedom

FREEDOM 5

Commencement
As fresh plasma graduates to the ground
Chalk line is rough as the chalkboard got broke up
This terrorism is not generational or conventional maybe
Provisional with the ignorance of forefathers that will
Land them in two places with both being permanent

Consistent as reminiscent of nightmares
Destructive warfare anywhere as
A bullet buries into a soul and
Fame is the goal? Nothing controls
I hate to rhyme so I intertwine

Good with the "Could have"
         "Should have"
         "Would have"

That's the proper hood way to say

If I coulda
If I shoulda
If I woulda

Voices varying as hallucinations haunt another Momma
Distraught as memories flaunt unstable, but unable to keep her legs
closed
Thought she had a "Man" misunderstand real men have plans not
contraband
To many syllables with babies on the County
Sanctioned in a situation that's unimpeachable
Dead will bury the Dead

Biblical revival as incarceration with no parole
Undernourished minds with unfamiliar times known as crimes
My career, my peers, and my fears the unwashed mouth cleared
I can't unfasten those living sins so no race ever hopes to win
Violence never rescinds, upset begging for peace
Her baby asks "when will Daddy be released?'

Freedom

FREEDOM 6

Clearance or clarity or confusion

As babies scream as they are tortured
The form of devitalized dreams
Craving attention with Momma's detention
Their only purpose is to be a visible byproduct to get public
assistance
I forgot about being formal
"On the County"

Statistics of institutions dependency as the screams continue to
poison
Burning his lungs with a sense of entitlement
Seeking nothing better survey generations as opportunities to
sequester
Her only asset is sprawled out as the janitor didn't mop
Where the horror of germs and motionless feet
Desecrate the floor the vulgar verbal pollution punctured his ears

"Mother_____"
"Ass____"
"Get up ...____"
Simultaneously she is called
"B____"
"S___"
"H_"

By the sperm carriers who become couriers
The next wild weeds of "Do Nothings"
Where does this cycle of apathy end?
Who is to blame? Government games
Does she know any politicians name?
All he will ever know is this neighborhood

He might see Disneyland or the beach
So many lungs and minds cry as they die
As different prisons populate with a hyperlink of time
She has no desire to educate just procreate
Every moment I hear those screams, my conscience yearns for
Any tomorrow with no more yesterdays

Today I hesitate, speculate or confer to... Freedom

FREEDOM 7

Confusion or chaos or criminals

Do these adjectives, verbs or nouns continue to?

Represent
Reflect
Neglect

The age-old adage that "Guns kill people"
                    "People kill people"
Demons drink from this delicious cup
To justify their reason for pulling a trigger
As the devastation is bigger the travesty lingers
The President steps to the podium breathing out

Senselessness as it's always the politics
It's never their loved ones for now, but how?
The world they know is privileged
No concern for mental health is this

Country
County
City
Neighborhood
Street
Household

A bottom feeder that doesn't get it
Wanting anyone in their mind to have it
(Life) so they'll

Shoot in Church
Shoot at Work
Shoot in School
Shoot at Home
Shoot up the Block
Shoot in the Park

These souls hated Dr. Seuss for the simplicity of it so murder the
innocent and guilty

Police Officer
Gangbanger
Boiling in a pot of terrorism
No one sees a solution just this
Conclusion
Confession

These cowards take themselves out of the equation
By death, jail or both accept the Police but that doesn't matter
Scenario _____ Lives Matter
After bullets cruise out of the chamber
Tearing through flesh with ferocity
Ceasing life as they knew it
We know them

By a sense of separation, the media (Social) consumes are brazen in their approach

Stop watching
Stop texting
Stop living selfishly

Is that carwash and barbeque legit?
Blood perfumes our psyche
I'm tired of writing these distorted dissertations
Waiting on to trust the answers that will finally come out your mouth

Freedom

FREEDOM 8

Church Sunday
ol English 800
Laying
Begging
Forgiveness
In fermented thoughts

Intent

As I drive by countless liquor stores
On every corner their religion is alcoholism
Commotion
Community
Convenience
The air is moist with anger

Invent

More demons make love to their psyche
Producing more chaos and embryos
Providing frequent excuses
Persistent panhandling
Belligerent behavior
Brilliant B__S___ bemoaning the inevitable

Instant

Schemes
Dreams
Demean

Freedom

FREEDOM 9

Crying or dying or lying

As Remi Reaper has a way of producing those tomorrows
that never come and all the wasted yesterday's simmer
like Grandmo's red beans...all day
how many loved ones, friends and "unknowns"?
Make love to chemicals moving decimals fueling that social utopia
as politicians can't control any truth

Every day, week, month and year is a lifetime

We witness another fallen soul wondering who is next
praying for a different concept
The tear bank foreclosed on bankrupted emotions

Social Media said you died but supplied
news with Reality TV storms washing any chance of privacy
Currents of torment take you under as an ocean of self-doubt

we tried to fish you out, but you went deeper
where I swam back to the surface of distrust
drug induced parents are absent as statistics

On the other hand I cannot understand
when champions overcoming challenges
As that bullet didn't know his name or future fame

Rendering his legs useless as he was (is) the embodiment of hope
Overcoming insurmountable odds of a drug induced nonparent
Foster care

Becoming a beacon and a hob nobbling with the Commander and
Chief
his village had raised him awaiting the reward... redemption
Now he prepares for a wheelchair as his body paralyzed but not his
mind

Easy for all of us to say today will these hurdles stifle his track
resolve?
I want to stop reading the paper watching the news
Listening to madness to stop to think that other societies lack
Freedom

FREEDOM 10

Social Media explodes with the fallout
Seeking the information my mind was "Burnt Out"
On senseless or useless causalities

I would follow this term "War"
No more
Is every day what we exist for?

Memories

What deity decides any human being must perish?
So you can be glorified as a terrorist to obtain
Free will or did they forget freedom has no debris

Their soul's desire hopes but deposit

Death
Destruction
Distance

Lives that mattered and did nothing to you
Peace is instant
Resistant
Irreverent
Life concurrent
To change

Freedom

EXIT EXODUS
11-20

FREEDOM 11

What starts this senselessness?
With another pointless killing of a Police Officer
No need to ask why the community gets lit up
He was a beacon to those who trusted him
His calling made him a Serviceman
Family man

Who doesn't mourn?
How do I still read the newspaper?
Watch the news?
Negative neglect pushed by positive views
With no clues to alleviate
Only the countless poison of nameless bullets

Simplified so there's no hope just dope to cope
Dispensaries misery as human life descends
A means to an end so no one comprehends
My hand trembles into a fist to resist
My mind reimburses those thoughts at a loss
Paying my psyche as you didn't care anyway

Freedom

FREEDOM 12

16 bullets

Bouncing off the suspicious street creating smoke
Into a lifeless, defenseless and unsuspecting body
A 3-inch knife with the misfortune of being

Worthless
Useless
Helpless

As the first round put him down as if he was an animal
Where's the conflict resolution? Crisis intervention
Reflection with no academy teaches the consequences

As news footage becomes an outcry

Payout
Sellout
Without

No amount brings his soul back
What could have been?
What should be? What would we see?

Tragedy
Blasphemy
Perjury

Freedom

FREEDOM 13

What will Hell be like?
Are we living it?
Am I judgmental?

Soul
Goal
Below

Not my responsibility so why do others feel they are judge,
jury and executioner
Who did some crime to them? Why kill? Why die?
For distain publicity as the innocent blood cries

Blame
Game
Same

I do not rhyme
Cry
Lie

In vain

Freedom

FREEDOM 14

Why?
What?
When?

Does this senselessness stop?
I keep writing to warn
Withstand these consistent whines

To ignorance that will poison
ruins
families
friends
strangers
enemies

Pray for peace that died centuries ago
War married indifference
Tolerance is a bastard and the illegitimate child of hope
Bullets burst bemoaning
Striking a defenseless soul as the truth
How they pay for the sins of others?

Brother (Brotha)
impact
Breathe

Sister (Sista)
all non-existent
Consistent and promiscuous

Mother (Baby momma)
Father (Baby daddy)
No compromise

Freedom

FREEDOM 15

Visualization
A can of beer as he grabs a pole
Pissing in the public toilet of life
Pissing away his dreams
Pissing into uncaring streets
Pissing from their subconscious

Observe
Deserve
Conserve

What little dignity he has left and don't forget to
Throw your trash out of a window of a moving car
Fight in the middle of the street
Male's vs. Males
Female's vs. Females
To become a social media celebrity for 5 seconds

Sista walks across the street with two babies in tow
"Watch where you going!" as a Momma screams "Damn it"
How can they watch where they are going?
When there's no light or wisdom
To see but they procreate for money and to inflict misery
Maybe future tragedies as perhaps

Public Assistance will take care of them
So to speak
All this weight hurts my back
My psyche
Little did I know this is?
Life is a plus or minus

Freedom

Freedom 16

Documentation
She lets a stranger rub her belly
In the assessment center maybe, she knows him
An unsuspecting Neighborhood Momma has again procreated
Another victim of no tomorrows a hard swallows
As he eats sandwich with no teeth
Maybe he's baby daddy, maybe he ain't

Her sandwich might be the only source of nutrition
That Victim Jr. gets today
She parades around as if she was in her mind in a
Beauty Pageant with high heels with no bra
Sundress as a toothless wonder continues to gum out his useless
dissertation
Sucking those gums while still running his mouth

There's no importance to his statements as
The main concern is another senseless birth or a fast track
Into the "'system" then the common question is
"Why was I born?"
It's an overblown scenario
With pretending Mommas

Grandma tries to keep them out the system
By raising them for the money
Hotel Jail vacations with anti-men now anti women too
I am desensitized to all of it
The generational genocide started on self-imposed despair
There's

Life
Death
Moments
Choices
Conclusions
Illusions

Freedom

FREEDOM 17 (ALI)

I had to think for a day or so to contemplate
Self-debate the term "Icon" is loosely used
Abused or confused with regularity rhymes to reason
There's no confusion or regulation of this man's

Soul
Spirit
Speech
Sermons
Entertained and educated before him our heroes were pigeonholed
into being a

Gentleman
Gracious
Giving

With him his bravado brushed your psyche
In fact, he was my parent's age they revolutionized together
Their generation had an impact as architects were assassinated
My Momma met him as he would order fish on Fridays
She didn't get a picture, but she got magic tricks, mystery
My Pop never betted against him

Scenario
Begging to sit in front the floor model TV in March 1971
The "Fight of the Century" sings, brings
A right hook that blasted his jaw
Witnessed momentum embrace a loss
The other half of the living room cheered
Smokin Joe smoked now who would he fear?

Their future lay in wait yet instigates
Two more Super Fights
Victorious in both but presets of vastness dictates
"Ali Boom Bye Yea"
That's how I heard it or imagined
All the wars he fought the warfare married strategy

Foresight
Fooling all of us as fools learn, yearn
Every time he fell we all got up
Never realizing there's always a means to an end

Comprehend
"I'm the Greatest of All Time!"
"I just shook up the World!"
"I'm a Bad Man!"
Permanent verbal markers to stamp and justify

Inspire
As a kid a put butterflies and bees in a jar
I thought I was enhancing floating and stinging
I got older so I begin to examine who he was
What he meant to be as seeing he was a

Poet
Prophet
Philanthropist
Preacher

Fighting Jim Crow round by round
Scarifying his freedom, career and manhood
Neighborhoods disrespected him for discarding his slave name
Demanding respect and dreaming of justice
Olympic gold medals don't float in the Ohio River
Rarely leaving an autograph seeker or small child
Dissatisfied as thousands of punches, sparring sessions and fights but
This opponent he couldn't cut off the ring or used
"Rope a Dope"

It's easy to claim he's a shell of himself
Doors opened as he made sure they would never close or
We begged for a quote or opinion on politics
Maybe his own sport as life as he knew it
We await another special tribute
As all of us have our own recollection

I have my memorabilia
My signed statute which only two exist
Watching old fights and his vernacular circus
Howard Cosell
Rubber Gorillas
"Rumble young man rumble...Ahhhhh!"

He refused to kill any Vietcong
The sport didn't kill him
Boxing kind of died when he left
There have been shooting stars but not a planet
As time is undefeated in one punch rings true
We all have a destiny waiting

Do you embrace it or run from it?

Muhammad Ali gave up his slave name
Cassius Marcellus Clay IV
Is the embodiment of?

Freedom

38

FREEDOM 18

Death

No one can defeat you or stop you
Only demons marry evil to love you
Social Media glorifies you

Our tears evaporate in the useless sun
My eyes continue to burn while
Wanting nothing more than cold emotions to eliminate the pain
Momma's babies continue to be lynched
With bullets instead of a rope
Flames of frustration fuel disgust
Her Bible has tattered pages with no mercy
Am I dancing around my words?
I am still waiting on our new future

Activist
Arch nemesis
Anti-hero

To slash this sexual abuse of power
While entrusted to protect and serve
Nearly a half century of

Who?
When?
Why?

If video doesn't convict?
If juries only try to acquit
Testimony is lies of transcript
As we selfishly offer up prayers
Is that not your son?
Brother, Nephew or Father

Are they going to slaughter a "Million Men?"
To counteract another march as well
Do these million men arm themselves?

C'mon Nat Turner
Sing Gil Scott Heron
Write James Baldwin
Dream Dr. Martin Luther King Jr.
Demand justice and maybe it's how we are asking
That's the wrong verb to those proper nouns are decorated glory

Clichés
Barbeques
Carwashes

I cannot imagine our ancestor's life
Hanging and burning with charred flesh
Welts of abuse, smells of indignity
To touch those scars for hope so
They been waiting, anticipating, and listening

Spirits wrestling with

Freedom
Free them

FREEDOM 19

Billows of smoke
Clouding my mind, psyche and memories
Billows of hope
Long divorced me and any person I care about
Billows of pain
Stabbing my nerves
Physically, mentally and spiritually
How many channels of this drama must I watch?

Listen to

Politicians
Preachers
Pimps
Players
Police

All attack from all sides

All day
All night
All my life

I can't read anymore
I can't feel anyone
I can't see anything

What do I write for?
When do the voices stop?
Why must I consume everything and nothing?
They cannot read, write or think
She was irresponsible to have sex with diseases
Her humanity commits treason

The baby cries burn his lungs
The breast milk he can't stomach
The truth is filled with poison
"I got this Momma"
"I didn't ask for this or her!"
"I know my future is going to Hell!"
He screams in the County Building
Counting on going into the system
His dreams of stability hoping
A prayer that someone will listen
He will run from bullets
Knowing some will hit him

Comprehend, defend
I will continue to rage with a pen
To document
This anger at the senselessness of society
Sobriety to remember those I blame
Ashamed as they're all bastard children of

Freedom

FREEDOM 20

Winter can't blow on me anymore because
It's not cold
I am that already that's why was I conceived
Irresponsibility
Selfishness
Need

That's not the case unless poverty is
Greedy
I can unsafely say no one helped me

The County
The Police
The Lord

Social Workers would come by to try
Just end up staying long enough to say
'I did my job" "There's nothing wrong here"
They didn't care if my soul got robbed as they had no
Rhymes or linger every time I was hit
Somehow I learned the phase, "You B____!" as I was

Starved
Abused
Neglected

The small closet danced in darkness as
My eyes couldn't adjust... trust the disgust
I ate what she (they) decided I can stomach

Feces, spoiled food, old milk, they gave me a bottle for my piss
"Drink up"
Pellets would bounce off my skin
The "Games of Ignorance" begin
Praying they graduate to guns
To end this horror against the summer sun
More rhymes with no reason
Motherhood was her treason
I couldn't bathe, breathe, and think as my lungs dried out from crying

Someone's God has been lying, trying
To assume I'll know a better Hell
Spring's pressure, this blanket itch... forever
Momma wants to play with me privately
With private parts as the emotional destruction haunts with
All the marks, all the scars, I am too young to be taken this far
My Brother and Sisters are lucky for I am the baby

Yet I get nothing
As the nightmares spit in my face every night

No school
No hope
No goals
No dreams
No future
No childhood

Not from these "Adults"
Age doesn't equate maturity especially
As I lay in this drawer

Ready to be cut and poked on by cause
Effect, regret, I feel no ill will towards anyone
No one knows as everybody saw someone should care
Now I guess I'm a statistic
Newspaper article which has a nice picture of my mother
Realistic as it shows the evil in her eyes but I have a different

Destiny
Tragedy
Mercy
My last sentence is
I am too inexperienced to write paragraphs
One word

Freedom

THOSE NUMBERS
21-30

FREEDOM 21

Crying
the streets are tearing up and cannot control
the flow of blood or tragedies
Crying
every day the media portrays some victim(s) being killed or murdered
Crying
with no color lines but the gray areas scale charts
towards black or nonwhite

Lying
Law Enforcement disturbing Justice, Jury and executions
Lying
as familiar cousins that abruptly and continually
abolished our ancestors
Jim Crow
Lynching
Dying
now instead of ropes the abuse, distain and torture
results now is a
trigger finger
poor training
insensitive
slaughtering hope as we are accustomed to being known as

Property
Sport
Entertainment

Shot while holding our hands up
Shot while following instructions
Shot while helping the disabled
Shot on hearsay
Shot for being "Black"
Shot for not being "African American"

When a Presidential Candidate states you get shot
in every Black neighborhood

Where is he?
Who does he see?
Why does this have to be?

When every Police Chief must investigate the senselessness

Who is he?
Where does he live?
Why don't they care?

When blatant racism is so systematic

Who are we?
Where are our dreams?

Violence is taught not inherited or is it?
cities cannot become communities of peace
only urban warzones so, this internal terrorism has manifested in

Physical
Mental
Spiritual

My Brother and Sister's keeper is transparent as
the Grim Reaper got shot while picking up more
shooters apparently, I cannot recount the countless martyrs
you know them as

Family
Friends
Nobody
Somebody
Enemies
Mercenaries

I just can't imagine this narrative reading this way
I understand, reprimand
yesterday, today, tomorrow
if I do not write another word
sentence, syllable, prose or paragraph
I have documented on my accord the undeniable cost of

Freedom

FREEDOM 22

Reality
Bit me in the ankles literally
I stepped out there (he or she) was
Sleep on the sidewalk
This normally does not bother me, but I am
Desensitized to the point of not seeing
This time I was concerned, what haven't I leaned?

Those human pieces of trash keep piling up
How does this keep happening continuously?

Rephrase
Praise
Raise

Do I accept scenarios as the norm?

Conform
Reform
Scorn

As one bathroom serves 1000 people actually
Every corridor is now housing
Tents make this first world country a third world misery
No community is safe, so they say and its
Possible solutions hear the same old rhetoric
He pissed in front of the Dollar Tree
Anywhere is now a toilet
No discretion for women and children as relief flows so easy

We accept it
Forget it
Never mention it

When the first word out of a politician mouth is
"We're going to build housing for the homeless"
Where is it? "We're going to provide mental health services to
Who? As benefits will be available for
Why lie? As I walk back the concrete serves as an unforgiving bed

He wraps his arm under his head as a pillow with
No covers, discover at the lowest common denominator
X doesn't equal

Freedom

FREEDOM 23

"I'm driving and recording because I'm doing me. Who is going to stop me...you? Don't b____ about what I'm doing cause there goes the Police right by and they weren't paying attention. What you worried about? Drive slowly and pray or speed up and hope I don't hit you. Either way I'll catch you coming or going. I'm living like that...wishes become you"

Impact
Crime
Time
Being young and stupid misappropriating embryos for uncertain
Futures the intrusion is irreversible and
Constantly "They gonna tear the Projects down?"

The screaming never listen just glisten
A bullet shines in another senseless death of lost souls
Drift from Hell to what the hell
Was Heaven considered in this picture?

Clearer as the TV blares with Reality TV
Three generations waiting on the number 4
To increase income (benefits) benefiting who?
Why live, love and work for any tomorrows
Todays, yesterdays that do not exist
On trust with only lives and lifetimes it matters after

Presidents act like children but you didn't vote for the privilege
Social Media has ruined innocence in the private us
Now any moment is filmed so we can view the

Demise
Destruction
Divorce

Cheating
Stealing
Ask for audacity

Of hope
Of dreams
Of consciousness

Marvin can't sing "Brother, Brother, Brother"
It's too late as No love is not here
Anyway but
By coincidence it
Would have happen already

The encampments are larger in every community

City
County
Country

Remember the 3rd world
We are the First Order
Disorder move over

Freedom

FREEDOM 24

I didn't ask for them God
Their relationship produced an embryo which became me
Otherwise I want to be in but nevertheless
My life was good at least I thought I was the link to them to

Love
Peace
Hope

Generations work that way, they promote family and futures
I never heard of Luis Sifer so who is he?
why is he dividing my family? when will he leave?
my Mommy and Daddy started

Fighting
Crying
Lying

On each other when the first one would ask a question
Leading to an accusation or arguments
This went on as a child my age I shouldn't see this
hear this, think this
Trust them or go with them

I started to split time between the two
each parent bad mouthing the other
the home as I knew didn't exist anymore
at last count, my sole purpose was a
Bargaining chip of course

I never heard of the word divorce
I was trying to grow up with some stability
I was now an actor in this reality screenplay
Each parent coached me on lying to the other
I didn't know what was true both were false
Daddy and I left the playground one day

I smelled gasoline
I smelled fear

I smelled trouble
Daddy said he should be better
my mistake was being tired of all the

Madness
Mayhem
Malfunction

I didn't believe or realize the blanket was wrapped around my neck
I watched Daddy press his hands on my throat

The air was gone as my life choked off
"What was Mommy going to say?"
"What was Daddy going to do?"
"Why did these two people get together?"

Daddy drove way out to the desert
Like he was going to Vegas this time he stopped and
Pulled my life stripped body from the back seat
Opened the trunk grabbing a shovel

I guess I was too much of a burden to get a funeral
the ground was extremely hot
As beads of sweat littered Daddy's face but disgraced
For a moment as he drove off

I thought Fathers were supposed to love their sons
I wanted to be like him, but I didn't know who he was
now I know he's a

Murderer
Monster
Man Less

The scenario went viral, local, national
 Mommy franticly searched for me
She didn't trust Daddy anymore
The Police found him bathing in alcohol and gasoline
Surprisingly I slept as if he created
This alternative universe built on inspection
Tore his non-truth down as evidence got him arrested twice

I met Mr. Conscience while lying in death
He said he will deal with Daddy
He always wins or he will torture his soul
True to form Mr. Conscience won a

confession
sentence
lifetime

The Social Workers hired to protect neglected their duty
Mr. Conscience has a date with them so no one wins
Mommy lost a child
Daddy lost his free life
I lost everything else
In the end I got the simple choice of

Freedom

FREEDOM 25

What adjective do I use now?
Anger
Frustration
Apathy
Fear
The reporters continue to report

Sort
Atrocities
Against the defenseless defending the living

Scenario
"Where's the gun?"
"We know where the bullets are."
"Why assume he's a criminal?"
"Will anyone see?"
Questions with answers
Answering no questions

Pacifying the neighborhood and bringing scapegoats
Watching a roast with a brunt offering of
Excuses with the usual bureaucracy
Accustom to lying, dying, trying to seek a justice while
Accusing Law Enforcement
Reruns get old but we will subconsciously

Watch
Listen
Learn

Lessons that still can't graduate only tragedy
Matriculates by losing sons
Fathers
Brothers
Leaders
Now innocent or guilty victims shown on documentaries

Souls God must evaluate as they're tormented
Are you helping by picking up the gun?
Problems explore wrong is wrong
Solutions right was right
This is not the last time this will happen
Life's TV never turns off as changing channels delaying the inevitable as

Candles burn out
Flowers wilt hustling
Barbeques for burials

Insurance
Assurance
Reoccurrence

Tomorrow stays ahead of us
Today is fogged in
Yesterday cries out over and over for

Freedom

FREEDOM 26

My ancestors didn't jump off that boat
They didn't fear bondage
They shouldn't have been enslaved
They behaved as King and Queens once now none

Citizens of a different nation twice
My children's generations choose to be
Socio- economical slaves demanding benefits that "Masta"
Said they can be eligible to as he put in parameters

Education
Childcare
Transportation

His cost as no one takes advantage
Not be at the risk of being comfortable
With not a drop of generational wealth with poor health
While others continue to pass us by

"Sell Out" if you make it
"Drop Out" is a badge of honor
Throw a "Get outta Jail" party
Apathy sits back and laughs at us with the souls of our ancestor's cry

It's easy for Momma to lie
"Why did Daddy die?"
Can't mourn a loss you didn't lose
Breathing for equality with inferior lungs
Full of illegal now somewhat legal weed
That neuron pickled with alcohol

What are they thinking?
We see hopeless tomorrows
Burning yesterdays
Scattered today, right there a difference
If we take that same enthusiasm
To see a fictional character applied it to

Learning
Earning
Voting

Now our ancestors jump for
Clouds can rejoice
As a voice reign

Freedom

FREEDOM 27

Where does it start? Will it ever end?
Familiar to comprehend
What "God" will do with these people?
Worship good or bad
Saint or Demon
Results are sad and trifling as it's no time for

Rapping
Rhyming
Reasoning

Obvious oblivions
21st Century Jim Crow
Have all of us whispering quietly
No Black Lives Matter
Only after disasters
Young Black Male Sympathy

Creates more tragedies
#Me-too but not today
How does an officer of?
Enforcement
Fear for his/her life from a
Fearful victim

Holding a cell phone
No a crowbar
From afar
Bullets didn't ask and they never do
Politicians will inquire
Conveniently with cruelty
Hoping we go away Social Media
Every day while newspapers are a foregone conclusion
Our splinter cells cry for

Uniting
Unity
Understanding

Grandmothers scream
Mothers scream
Daughters scream

Our children they demean as
All neighborhoods are one crisis
Sacrifice to pretend to be nice
In saving some lost with zero cost

"Sweep the homeless away with my tax dollars"
"Guns don't kill people"
As obituaries can't say enough
Praying for insurance
Instead of carwashes and barbeques as the famous

Preacher
Pastor
Minister

Steps to the podium
Expounding million-dollar words
50 cents phrases are all we hear
"Why does he have that badge?"
"There are only a few bad apples"
"Why is he still on the force?"

Just as the human travesties take more lives
At least these cowards don't kill themselves
Hiding behind "Blue Walls of Justice?" so their conscience should do
that
Their souls sleep with nightmares producing mind altering embryos
Lies or the truth never mattered after all our ancestors knew all too
well
Jumping and drowning meant swimming with

Freedom

The shackles clang to a Negro spiritual
My ancestors labored by asking for
Mercy maybe somehow
Someway they knew a better tomorrow
Existed despite their timeless death
Raped at all levels while lynched by smiling devils
Believing God told them

Generations live for survival
Creates a revival so my pen to page
Rage engages Freedom

FREEDOM 28

Moist crisp nature is unnatural
Urban renewal
Gentrification tool
Cruel as thousands live on concrete
Blankets, tents, and tarps for the

Hopeless
Homeless
Helpless

The uncertain buzz of politics, critics, misfits
"Not my neighborhood."
"They bring my property value down."
"You're not building shelters here"
Gentrification grinds, unwinds
Eliminating the terminology of

Ghettos
Slums
Hoods

Makeshift dwellings can't hold out water, bugs, Police
Upgraded bus stops became pseudo apartments
Until they removed the benches

After the iron bars didn't stop sleep
Public doesn't cry for this humanity
Different nomads live in a citizen's world
Devoid of rhetoric elected mouths spew excuses
At least they are consistent, reminiscent
Why my race was emancipated
Where did they go? Back to Masta
To "Sharecrop"
On top of no benefits as economic nothing

This country pledged allegiance not to care
"They don't pay taxes!"
"They can live somewhere else."
"I'm tired of walking over them."
When did our society decay to this point?
When they voted to say it's legal to smoke a joint? Or is it?

Divorcing minds
Souls
Situations
Include time
How many articles need to be written?

To state the obvious
"I have a right!"
Responsibility
Respect of

Freedom

FREEDOM 29

You will not serve me
I will not patronize your business
Standoff as purpose

Conclusion
Solution
Infusion

Jim Crow impregnates their psyche as he
Terrifies our humanity
Indefinitely

Hands up!
Shoot
Hands down!
Shoot
Handcuffed
Shoot
Traffic stop
Shoot
Domestic violence
Shoot
Skin color
Shoot
"I fear for my life!"
Shoot

Homicide
Genocide
Collide

Can we coexist without Law?
Enforcement lawless
With modern day lynching's
Reminiscent of terror our ancestors

Faced as when us as a race is erased
His future by hanging his tomorrows
Testifying or justifying
Jim Crow as a Savior

While burning emancipation to form a
Different Hell or tell us we are not a citizen as you say we are
Three fifth American
We were shipped here unwillingly

Yet we still want to be true as

Any skin color matters
Why should multiple rainbows open the sky?
Blind eyes see nothing what type of buffering will I have to deal with?

My Grandchildren must know
My Grandparents survived you Jim Crow
Their life lessons influenced me
For scenarios when I was the only
Representative of my race
The looks on their face

Persecution
Problems
Poverty

When will we see non-ethnic tomorrows?
Can we bury yesterday?
Today has little chance

Glance
As I
They
She
He
Romance

Freedom

FREEDOM 30

Souls burning
Learning
Searching

For a cool wind gust of hope
Against a backdrop misled by selfishness panic aggravation
no one will listen, in fact some will
Kill so mill over the white noise playing in them
mind games coping chemicals, he copped during a
Out of control with psycho logic rage in his mental cage

Preparing to mix more demons with intent
Harm him and/or others to self-medicate
date and relate as no one care
He finds a sidewalk bed as the tarp keeps out the world of
Deceit on dirty concrete seeping into his subconscious life
Strife with sacrifice means my today is intact

So many questions with no answers as he lied, died and tried
To comprehend conditions he didn't deserves
It's cold tonight as a warm tomorrow doesn't matter
Another injection will tune him or her up
after a legal smoke as Dr. Cannabis states
"Laws are a joke so it doesn't choke."
Society must investigate, interrogate
or infiltrate negative moratoriums
They wanted better a while ago goes to show
All this human trash will be swept up with no positive ending
They piss on America take a dump on Liberty

Spit on Freedom

NEIGHBORHOOD-LOGY
31-40

FREEDOM 31

Cry about as spirits shout
Dissenters doubt
He made millions off rhymes

Lines
Adjectives
Nouns

Concur to the obvious oblivion with ignorance
Selfishness with disrespect
Now we are once again subject to

Incarceration
Brutality
Injustice

Once again, our skin color marinates prejudice
Seeds of Social Media where any statement is publicized
We all claim 15 seconds of infamous fame to those who entertain

Artist
Athlete
Activist

The real enemy is depression, drugs with disposition or confederacy
Do we have a responsibility? To at least uphold what minuscule
gains we earned
Crosses burn. Choices learn as souls continue running with no
manifestations of tomorrow
We are living for our ancestors today as yesterdays are on their
striped backs, loins and psyche

It's always someone who we thought stood with us
That shanks us in the back or was he misquoted
What he said authentic?
Did brainwashing take place?
Judging motives only distorts whatever truth is out there
Disappointments disallow positive scenarios
Bones in oceans can't swim with mouths of this society with
Publicity

Fallout
Free speech = Free dumb

Freedom

"Now that this ignorance is out there where does that leave me? My mouth didn't listen to my brain so I hit send. Y' all wanna crucify me now, I'm speaking my truth... I think. I get to say what I wanna say in this country. I got money, fame and celebrity so kiss my ass and step off. I'm not taking anything back for nobody..."

Is this where we are? Quoting fictional characters
The icons of justice meant more, sacrificed more
Loved more died once

Only to be re-killed by deception
No inspections or transgression
Multiply lies
Trust disgust
Are avenues making left turns on?
The right side of right

Freedom

FREEDOM 32

Atrocities
Adjectives

Descriptions lost in the narrative
Citizen in America is an
Immigrant voluntarily or involuntarily asylum
Forfeits the Land of opportunity my ancestors had their children

Snatched
Sold
Stolen

What's the difference?
They didn't ask to come to become
Indirectly

Slaves
Servants
Silenced

Each century has the same insane
Results expecting a different outcome
Only the skin color is reminiscent as a justification of

Lynching
Lunacy
Lying

Those trees know when those souls whine
That rope still has skin in its twine
This America is not minding its business

Now children scream out losing all trust
They be treated as animals in the 21st century
Concentration camp conveniently
The messenger sounds like the same interpretation
History ravages our minds devoid of time
Sad part is we put "Him' there

By voting or not voting
Democracy divorced us
No reconciliation either
Neither person wants better however
Letters on paper form no words or sentences
Empty as they came out of their mouths

Grandmo always said
"Can't do better if you don't you're think better."
Social Media created these monsters
We all can speaker indulge in

Fame but if we speak and seek scenarios
That fall on deaf post text, emails simultaneously
The "Hell Express" speeds down those treacherous tracks
Spirits riding want the last stop to read an obituary of foolishness

Freedom

FREEDOM 33 (NIPSEY)

These Superheroes are not reborn
their Endgame is permanent
tragedies everlasting
violence is a cruel lover full of hate
He knows no creed or color in South LA
Lost Angels are Devils of

Deceit
Destruction
Devastation

Tearing away the fabric of

Hope
Dreams
Happiness

The few seconds of sending that projectile
forward turns all the progress backwards as rising evil
now masquerading as a memorial
Most Souls have good intentions
Many souls have bad interventions
Until the next Hero falls

Someone calls the lessons unlearned burn in fact
That happened already twice as negative embryos continue to
Harvest senselessness just as we Marvel at our Heroes
They were reborn from the fruit of those life lessons
Failure, mistrust and ignorance and a lack of faith but their pages
turned while
Not quitting believing as is so they rewrote their story

They're not Captain America
They're South LA
Yearning for the technology of Tony Stark
To revitalize the renewal

Its clean playgrounds and its nice strip malls
It's low-income housing for these visions see until
Apathy cries in a different multiverse
Disrespect doesn't exist but you are a Man of Principle
Substance respect as the extended hand pulling up Humanity
Helping those who can't help themselves

Children
Elderly
Homeless

Reality that escapes most by omission and commission
With chemicals, alcohol and deceit as these living nightmares have
no ending
The day to day struggles is dirty tap water, trash, tents and piss
stained allies
PTSD for the Superheroes who lived for others
The issues will continue to define them or
We could become the Heroes why do we run away avoiding the?

Earth
Rebirth
Renewal

Starts long before the funeral
Are we thinking while grieving?
Do we love one another?
Are just deceiving everyone
We are all sick of the obvious with all the candles
Vigils won't avenge these Heroes or provide

Freedom

P.S.
The Marathon continues as your uniqueness must live on
Your pages will be read with the investments you made paid
Dividends in the neighborhood you loved

Peace, Faith & Blessings

FREEDOM 34

I can lie to you as I could
Bribe you as I should
Tell the masses any truth about
Negative embryos
Navigate ignorant scenarios
Contempt hunger so respect justice
If the last few years taught us anything
Nothing is sacred anymore ...before

Peace
Kindness
Love
Hope
Pain
Life

Blame Social Media or media is antisocial
Fact is this is not a multiverse of realities
Those situations no one wants to take care of
The fruit that grows as you piss on that
Still feeds souls and controls goals
Your narrative is either "Steel or Velvet"
What Genesis or Revelation
Do you have to offer?
Whatever or whoever and why this impact

Freedom

FREEDOM 35

Momma
Who?
How?

I am old enough to ask why you wouldn't take Daddy back.
In fact I thought you wanted the best for me
See the difference between blood and truth
Am I in need of wisdom, guidance with hope?

I just started living as my life was a scant speck regrets as I'll miss
being 7, 10, 18 or 21
I won't learn how to drive or play basketball maybe be the next
LeBron
Graduate from High School, college or have a girlfriend or start a
family
With my own babies because I'm a baby myself
Well you decided to put your trust in another man
I didn't understand you said I needed a man to raise me

Did you hate Daddy that much?
You loved one another once you said he was good with children
Not your child, the pain was so I didn't know what did I do? My body
screamed
This is way beyond what I knew while lying with confusion
Conclusion is adults always try to fix a different truth as he couldn't
stop his

Anger
Aggression
Apathy

All the increments of another tragedy as I lay praying
In my nightmares and prayers why does everyone stare?
Momma did you care?
Now I'm on the news with Coach as my pictures started an inquiry

Testimony
Reality
Stolen
Misbegotten

So where's my

Freedom... Momma is done

FREEDOM 36 (JOHN LEWIS)

Icons are born and consciousness is learned

His America
My America
Is not our America

Never was or
Never will be with
No optimism just truth
He was willing to fight
Ready to fight
Not with his hands but his insight
To get in "Good Trouble"
Necessary trouble
He lived this as a theory

Jim Crow didn't destroy him
Jim Crow can't destroy us
He's a byproduct of racism's mistrust

The tool was nonviolent civil disobedience
Jail meant victory
A bridge of racism couldn't stop him
His body battered but not his spirit
Oppression continues to suffocate
Yet he stood for change without hesitation
Sometimes a purpose can lead to perseverance
Trained by the Drum Majors for peace
He always beat that drum

I'm beating that drum until my hands are raw
Bleed as justice
Honor of voting
Respect is speaking with no regrets
Activism, with integrity caged
By his morality is our legacy

Freedom
The Boy from Troy earned his

Freedom 37

Hell has been here as society is hit with these paradigms

In my apartment minding my own business = dead
Sleep in my apartment bothering on one = dead
Stopped with my hands up = dead
Jogging my neighborhood = dead
Knee on my neck = dead
Getting in my car to avoid drama = near dead

If you do not know the common denominator
Then you're part of the problem
We have been and will remain a worthless entity as others are alarmed

Age or social status does not stop these lynching's
That hood has been replaced with a badge and gun
This is the horror our ancestors faced
Their souls mourn
Their hearts heavy with the continued reality of
This senselessness manifested so we have

No Freedom

FREEDOM 38

The smoke of protest burns our lungs
That was some Momma's son
Brother
Father

There are always "Thoughts and Prayers"
I care that these Demons are inclusive
Elusive or abusive being non-apologetic to women

They are not immune neither are their children
Our ancestor's scars didn't heal injustice but trust this
The rope is tightening by fear as those
Hands are covered in sinless blood
Sick of Jim Crow committing these atrocities of 403 years
With millions of lynching's

Actual systematic notches on his ledger
Your tears mean nothing
Something to Humanity's ears

Freedom

FREEDOM 39

I'm tired of running as
My ancestors say different
Survived different
Times were different
What's chasing me?
I see

Pessimism
Police
Pandemic

What's scaring me?

Bullets
Brutality
Broken promises

Some mornings you want the darkness of night
Most nights you want the beginning of day
I'm confused all the time
Can my mind, body and spirit should be in one accord
These Demons chew at my psyche
They're Hell bent on destroying me

Freedom

FREEDOM 40

7
The number equates to 11
Use to say Heaven to balance the minutes
Now it's the number of bullets with no rhyme or reason
Fired into another back of a Black Man

In front of his children that horror is rinse and repeat
Those "I am a Man" posters of the 1960s
Burned along with the hope of respect
Didn't we earn that? No

Try to do right = Shot
On a bike or drop a gun = Shot
Run away from trouble = Shot
Fight for your country = Shot

4
Victims killed by a young Racist
What are we going to do about that?
Nothing in fact
He's a Patriot and I do not mean a football player
Claimed he was defending business
From another state
This behavior is taught as his Momma initiates
Ignorance

He walked in front of the Police with his weapon = Not Shot
Claim some "Black Man" is threatening him = Not Shot
Listen to the so called "Leader of the Free World" = Not Shot

As my fist remained balled up as my mind cannot process
This Hell has no end with no tomorrows coming
Or going but somebody better get a handle of this

Freedom

OBSERVE MY REVELATION
41-48

FREEDOM 41 (BREONNA TAYLOR)

We knew it was coming that feeling
As your stomach and heart drops
As the specter of Jim Crow's 400 years of

Lynchings
Beatings
Shackling

Rises again firing bullets into our women
Who did nothing but be the best version of her
She wasn't exploiting the system
Exploiting children
Exploiting herself
Just contributing to the positive members of society

Law Enforcement which no one trusts
Embolden by a system seeded in hate a must
That never works for us against everyone of color (us)

The hired Klan sworn to protect and serve
Another dose of poison we don't deserve
We're tired of this learning curve
Their math: 32 shots + 3 officers = 1 dead
The walls got justice
So did her neighbors

Our ancestors continue to watch in horror
We're trying to represent them with honor
Seems as if our lives are not worth a dollar

Prejudice will not retire so those hoods are easy to hire
As each martyr's death should inspire
The streets are buckling under the weight of the protest
Of course, no one seems to know what's best
Demons will never confess
Sorry is never near a protest

Every aspect of our existence is bathed in fear
A Motown Anthem would make it clear
Justice is blind and continues to disrespect us
Injustice can see and still kills us
No justice is where Jim Crow wants us
Pure disgust
Somewhere
Somehow
Some way
We will get us
Some

Freedom...say her name...Breonna Taylor

FREEDOM 42

Water or piss
As I walk out the steel enforced door towards the sunlight
With a puddle under her to confer

I didn't want to waste the mental excursion
On another sad soul who now treats society as a toilet
The pandemic but these lifeless embryos were already
Destroying society

Who hasn't seen piles where you wonder if that was a dog?

Do you try to desensitize yourself?
No point calling for help

Why does this bureaucracy allow this chaos?
No point calling for help

How do you clean our society up and restore it?
No point calling for help

When will we listen to Momma Nature?
No point calling for help

Where will the focus come from with everyone doing better?
No point calling for help

After working for decades with this mentality
I have concluded
No more psychological transfusion disputed

Just

Freedom...Period...*I'm calling for help*

FREEDOM 43

The psychosis of a monster is attacking in her head
As she screams with permission's love crying and asking to be dead
Early morning pilgrim on a dysfunctional street corner
Cars and neighborhood Zombies move on ignoring her disorder

This screaming Sermon became a bitter testimony
Sadly no one could offer anything or nothing
The intensity of her yells bemoans as they belch out
Some inquiry was just to verify without a doubt

The unfair air was crisp with fiery smoke
A mental photograph swims like sharks biting at folks screening a
pitiful joke
She can't cover up years of dirty neglect
A piss stained blanket mixed with mental illness and substance
abuse got no respect

This profanity is not to encourage being profane
It's a cry for the levels of help that became insane
We can run from this phantom pretending there's no need
Harmonizing against the respect as you proceed

Truthfully, that could be anyone of us
Which situation in your life do you trust?
Unfortunately as we continue to see all of them
Another tragic example of a soul begging for

Freedom

FREEDOM 44

Nightmares start off as innocent dreams
Nightmare's anger burns hot so it seems
His dreams can turn into a nightmare
But his mind's eye is not aware or scared

If he's trying to rhyme or reason
Just to commit subconscious treason
His mouth can't belch out an answer
Rude speech no one brave can master

His soul was burned by the sunlight
Those goals were lit by a dark moonlight
As his thoughts attacked his words
His war made him again sound absurd

Where does his non tomorrow begin?
Those real yesterdays have some more sin
So today he knew he couldn't win
He takes all the cannabis smoke in

His false starts with fast times were getting lost
He thought he was a boss with no real cost
Only this bureaucracy continues to sustain him
In his mind democracy continues to abuse him

Now his life thesis is a sad joke
He can't evaluate any form of hope
Wasted large portions of time on the worst of him
This ignorant ocean of drama won't allow him to swim

As blind ambition is specific but needs no permission
His language of profanity is off course in transition
The undercurrent of his truth affect poor decisions

Freedom

FREEDOM 45

A thunderstorm of knowledge I didn't get
My washed-out mistrust of hope you will regret
The love we try to do is always suspect

Can't get out of my own way

Clouds of mismanagement rain nothing
At least sunshine could offer something
All these days I burn out with nothing

Can't get out of my own way

A mental shower will not cleanse me
My clear mind is smoked in misery
You would figure any non-soul believes

Can't get out of my own way

Billows of foolishness create embers
Not one thought is a chance to remember
Earth, Wind & Fire sang hits in September

Can't get out of my own way

Someone will get a pen to page rage
My proof lives in a different cage
Funny how you can't achieve with no age

Can't get out my own way

Freedom

Damn it
Free me

FREEDOM 46

Every day you open your eyes it's your birthday
I'll preach it or teach it
Can I examine every word that comes belching out?
Your mouth literally
Trust me really
See

The new dissertation you presented
Has misrepresented
Your muted objective
Truth kills a lie as another embryo cries

The union was senseless
Simply to fill a need
Other methods could serve
Instead of collecting seed

Scenarios deserve
An outcome or don't say
You'll do better and say please
You don't know all 26 letters

There's a word
Subtle verb
Adjective
Sentence that will formulate

Freedom
free me

FREEDOM 47

This world forced him into a Pen to Page rage
He wanted his own pen name now he's enraged
He's running against another sad destiny today
But somehow he'll write to acquire to earn his stay
These creative nightmares make him crazy
Those thunderstorms don't accept him being lazy
Almost sixty years of his ancestors' clout
Those voices said get out

Ol Big Momma on a defunct street corner
Different embryos coming from somewhere
He must document so someone will care
Now they're wild weeds going nowhere
All we can do is be blind to their stare
Just another police murder to happen any way
When will we start to make these monsters pay?
Does our story count for a renewed hope anyway?
That voice says get out

She yells "I know this is their America"
It's no longer the land of fantasy
Tell them, teach them, and help them
That my ancestors didn't die for nothing
With a pen in hand he'll say
In a hopeful way
Freedom please

Ol Big Momma walking through the Hood
You spit at this generation
It's not their fault they're left to try
Thoughts are imagination boiled in time
They screamed "save me"
His pen to page rage scribbled
Get out

Ol Big Momma on the Project's doorstep
Did your Baby Daddy get out of jail yet?
She needs another stimulus check
Keep praying there are safer bets
Her dishearten voice shouts
"Lawd have mercy for my babies"
After 400 years of our ancestor's doubt
They cried get out

She recounts "Where is our America?"
She was raped by treachery
Better worry while overseeing this truth

His pen is his eyes to a difficult curiosity
He'll make them pay or declare his fame
One day or one way
Freedom please

Free me

FREEDOM 48

Sad snow melting in the ignorance of your truth
Sunshine is not tomorrow
A piece of today or two hours of yesterday
Why did my ancestors try?
No more pain to buy
No weeds can bloom in promise so why?

Without a reason its dying season
Causes nothing but emotional treason

Freedom is power not slavery

My miracle is the best version of me
It's not a starburst only I can see
The empowerment is clean as an anti- sky
Many mothers have no more tears left to cry
This thesis will not abandon our pride
I need pursuit to swim between the lines
Call me what you want: Negro, African American or Colored
Those ancestors scream because I can't rebuff it
At least I'm not cussing or saying _____ it

I finally have a sense of voice
to manifest a different choice

Freedom is power not slavery

Your beginning is not my end
We all have repercussions to defend
I dated and married poetry
Lifetime lover of destiny
That audience wants to speak
Advocacy running over hot coals with callusing feet
Honoring sentences of forefathers
Their unapologetic stance made them bother
My ambition will carry them further
Your knowledge will make my story clearer

Freedom is power not slavery
Free me mercy

FREEDOM SONGS

Freedom Song 1

Creating is my business
Writing is my business
I'll create as a business
I'll write as a business

Leave other writers works alone

To each its own
That's my philosophy
I want to write for you
You want to write for me

Write every day, do your thing
Create anyway, do your thing
Always remember

Creating is my business
writing is my business
I'll create as a business
I'll write as a business

Leave another artist work alone

To each its own
That's my philosophy
I want to write for you
And you want to write for me

Write what you say, do your thing
Create your way, do your thing
Always remember

Creating is my business
Writing is my business
I'll create as a business
I'll write as a business

Leave other poets work alone

To each its own
That's my philosophy
Will you write for you?
I'll write for me

Freedom Song 2

Freedom is power
pain
poison
pleasure
peace
passion

Intelligence
instruction
institution
understanding
underwhelming
unity

Earned through blood
sweat
tears
peers
trying to clear
their conscious fears

Diligence
dignity
desire
devoid
deliverance
decisions

Claims a community
in suburbs while
urban neighborhoods are
misunderstood
Rebel
in another Ghetto

I'm writing this book
for overlooked eyes of
my ancestors
my tragedies
my enemies
A prose speaks truth differently

Free them
Free us
Free me

FREEDOM SONG 3

Angry epiphany
Toxic ignorance
Killing Humanity, remember him?

Falsely accused of being a human being
That phase loses its humane quality
As Humanity cries against himself

Those proper adjectives preach
Bigotry, hatred, prejudice as racism
Is lying while my world is dying

The breath I can't catch
Leave my lungs broken
My ancestor's legacy a token
Humanity cries against me

There are no clouds of hope
Only thunderstorms of discontent
Now the sunshine is hollow, what's left to beg for?
The reflection of burnt glass shines Humanity

This rain only washes in fear
My psyche drowns in fifthly water
My soul floats endlessly with no direction

Somehow, some way I'll rise
Blow the horn Herb Alpert
One year does not make a lifetime
Until your years are pawned off
A novel better version of me
Will battle against these reading calamities

One word
One theme
One chance

Freedom

FREEDOM SONG 4

My eyes water in a burning sea of anger
My faith has nothing to do with this

I'm sick of Law Enforcement shooting us
I'm tired of thoughts and prayers
I'm sick of belched excuses
I'm tired of protest in jest
I'm of sick of Politicians lies
I'm tired of begging for respect

I ask for peace as I pray
I cry for silence against black noise
I ask for hope with healing
I try to maintain sanity
I ask for clean tomorrows
I cry from dirty yesterdays

We are better than this
They do not believe we are
We are living with our ancestor's weight
They refuse to acknowledge them
We cast a ballot no one honors
They blame everything on us

Where is the Love is an old R& B song?
I can't find meaning or any sense of right
I don't want to swing low with no goals
There's nothing to gain by rising high
The middle is nowhere but a waste
I'm just wanting to be normal or equal

One time
One mind
One grind

Freedom

FREEDOM SONG 5

Interrupted disturbance
All our being is violated by disobedience
Rivers of violence washes
Our narrative away as self-trust is drowned
Time tested lies which cost innocent lives
This scenario renders noncompliance

We cling to impatience where's no answer
No one cares to be patient causing disasters
Our thoughts are littered with rhymes, reasons
There's no need to have a prerequisite to this revolution
Those foundations are sandy but weaken
That is the situation not the solution

Harold Melvin told the Blue Notes to Wake Up Everybody
How many seasons will we slumber through?
If we don't start learning where's strength?
Extend your heart out then your mind will follow
They preach to the wrong church choir
We invest in the tabernacle of hope

One word
One noun
One sound

Freedom

FREEDOM SONG 6

Someone I admire said
Life is a collection of memories
Comprised of love in pain and loss
I had to take inventory of this statement
I'll get a residual from the resentment
There's no resolution or conclusion needed

Who will be honest in their truth?
Who will offer peace?
Who will promote forgiveness?
Who will shed the light on hurt?
Who will offer gifts to Humanity?
Who will be in their right mindset?

Can you embrace love as life?
Can you be a better version of yourself?
Can you trust hope to see it though?
Can you measure respect as a necessity?
Can you exhale on that moment?
Can you inhale those thoughts?

Two days
Two nights
Two eyes

Freedom

FREEDOM SONG 7

I pulled on a thread of America
Its fabric rips apart into burnt pieces
The callous embers melted my vision
With some pretense which included illusion
Those picket signs have punished me
With brutality yet "What's Goin on"

An Anthem is needed to expand the willingness to cope
No one listens so why widen the adversity of the scope
This apathy chokes my perspective
Rendering a negative objective

Where does this leave us?
Floundering in multi-verses of despair
If we were sheep looking at a wolf
The first bite is where the terror is

I can turn around to run towards the Shepperd
Now I'm guaranteed a future with hope
Applying knowledge with faith and understanding
The air must freshen positive

Four lines
Four times
Four cries

Freedom

FREEDOM SONG 8

Who is killing Humanity, remember him?
He is or was supposed to help us
He can't help himself
Demons of mistrust beat the Hell out of him

Everyday my soul is shot
Everyway my goals are stolen
Everyday my soul is worthless
Everyway my goals are rendered meaningless

How come we continue to struggle with race?
How come we defer as they lie to our face?
How come we repeat this senseless case?
How come we are accused of stirring up the base?

Humanity is better than this
Humanity will never dismiss
Humanity says rain is not piss
Humanity knows life is hit and miss

Five sunrises
Five sunsets
Five regrets

Freedom

FREEDOM SONG 9

That ugly racially blood-stained window
Was cleaned as the minority janitors
Swept up the glass while it's their job as those
Words with phases soaked into our consciousness

Nothing for my ancestors as I can only think of
The unspeakable horror they endured
Many of us thought if the skin color is different
Then we are not having this conversation

These unpopular proper nouns germinate
Domestic Terrorist
Insurrectionists
Thugs/Rioter/Hoodlum

This mob mentality is centuries old lynching's
It's the birth of Jim Crow to stop reconstruction
It's the Edmund Pettus Bridge
It's the blatant misuse of this judicial system

More clouds of ignorance will form
Raining the bitter acid of contempt
Soaking this country's sidewalks with hate
That fifthly water washes away nothing

We paid for patience for no privilege
We know better but we continue to examine
We'll never forget or can't afford to refine
We've seen "Birth of a Nation"

This time
These crimes
Those lies

Freedom

FREEDOM SONG 10

I watch every morning as I drive by those tents
I listen to the cries of chaos, piss or repent
Homelessness
This word is used in the same vein of profanity
No one says it or no one wants it
No one cares to help and no one gives a damn

I turn away when one decides the sidewalk
as a toilet offering no rinse
I cannot comprehend the understanding
Officials who continuously lie about that
Where's the funding that can stop this menace?
Where's the reform that will prevent this Hell?
Where's the empathy to think of others?

No Messiah will come for their merciless souls
They can't save themselves, we can't either
Their lives have been a pandemic as they rot as a human disease
Widespread over this entire society
cause and effect are senseless lies no one protects
Those solutions will continue to be suspect

The trash washes over the neighborhood
Their seashore eroded with chemicals
to dull this range of indifferent pain
We try to help but our voices are silenced
by red tape, white fear and blue noise
Why not offer an equal opportunity? no color lines
Why not offer some serious counseling? mental crimes
Why not offer to throw away their dreams? selfish times

Their situation is pathetic
When do these Politicians stop scheming and cheating?
How is this the Greatest Country on Earth?
How would you like to be the worst person in America?
Turning one America against the other
Brewing a cauldron of racism, hate, bigotry and prejudice
Despite having the title of Democracy of the Free World

If you understand there are two Americas
Privilege vs. discrimination = lawlessness/disruption
Affluent vs. poor = disparage
Harmony vs. tragedy = senselessness

There are no true "Americans" but the natives, right?
Indigenous with no knowledge of what was coming
Slaughtered by being judged beneath "them"

The inhumane massacres continue to build this country
Rendering their people defenseless as they tried to defend
Only to end up on reservations supposedly sovereign

This country's history is a masquerade of lies
We are not taught two different histories
The miss-education begins with slavery
Employment and protection to benefit
Emancipation was supposed to bring reconstruction
That lie brought sharecropping with Jim Crow

They lynched my ancestors but what happened to yours?
They burned down "Black Wall Street" but the other one?
They continuously keep shooting us and you?
You got to breach the Capitol as we saw

My ancestors lived their lives in terror for their future
Generations to survive as we live in their memory
Your privilege affords luxuries and provisions
While you're elected bureaucrats belch mistruths

Your misogyny raped my Grandmothers
You mistreated those generations
In any inquisition there was never a mistrial
Because in your mind it was a misunderstanding

As we bare witness to this reoccurring horror
Not wanting to believe what we are seeing
Now we comprehend, know who you are electing
This ignorant fable will continue repeating
I'm waiting for those words "Thoughts and Prayers"
Neither will be taken seriously, in fact who cares
I realize this damage my Grandchildren will see
They're not born yet but already paying

Cast your vote
Cry for hope
Clean with soap

Freedom

FREEDOM'S FREEDOM

FREEDOM'S FREEDOM 1

My Pop was born in 1941 the same year as Emmitt Till
His uncle lived in Chicago as he was raised in Louisiana
What if my Grandfather sent him to Chicago in the summer of 1955?
What if he saw the Demon who lied to the innocent?
What if the unspeakable horror befell my Pop?
There's no me or any of my siblings or my children

As we as a race continue to suffer with these atrocities
As an experiment in the human narrative, when does it end?
After countless souls are executed as a modern form of lynching
Lifeless goals wash away in an ignorance of ignorance
How much can a persecuted psyche take?
Why do mothers have to bury their children every day?

What happens if we rebel, stand up or speak out as they did?
We know the answer and know not to ask that question period
If you must ask without an answer, your part of the problem
Unconsciously you do not see or want to believe or understand
How many times must this "Twilight Zone" come on for you?
As "Art Imitates Life" with no channel needed

Who is supreme over whom? A race that enslaves another?
This supremacy has not allowed that race to recover from
This apocalyptic atmosphere, that's their story not ours to tell
The senselessness of announcing you're better, for what?
It stands to reason as you lied, cheated, killed and stolen
Now you feel that you can overthrow democracy

You have no intent of ending this chaos
It hangs around your neck as an albatross
Our heroes knew what bridges to cross

Freedom's Freedom

FREEDOM'S FREEDOM 2

Forsaken now devoured
What does democracy mean?
It's just a word in too many sentences
My ancestors were strangers to this land
Enslaved as cargo then sold as a commodity
Chains were the first handcuffs to shackle

There's no milk and honey for us
We turned discarded scraps into meals
Did any history book teach you this?
My ancestor's soulful voices were spiritual
They were beaten by vicious race fueled rituals
Now those bullets are black for a reason

I'm sick of so-called humans opening their soiled mouth
The unmitigated stench of habitual lies continues to poison
This unprotected climate will burn every citizen
Those elected to help are complaisant in this Hell
They celebrate the ceremony of death regardless
They are innocent souls at rest in a burial parking lot

When will this nightmare turn forward?
More salt with destruction melts backward
Someone always preaches loud we will rise
Then an indifferent cloud hits the sunrise
Do we continue to witness mindless rebuttals?

Saying we're better than this is not nearly going to be enough
Rebuilding shattered hopes, dreams, and lives will be possible but
rough
Humanity will eradicate the senseless sins of the corrupt

Freedom's Freedom

FREEDOM'S FREEDOM 3

Destructive ignorance is not bliss but it's dangerous
Now tragic, senseless and I remiss but it's suspicious
The stars reject light to this worthless endeavor
Any moon respects night which no one treasures
Why destroy the one Republic that needs Freedom?
This megalomaniac can con and placate them

We already know if you darken in tone what would happen
Historic rise cannot suffer casualties
My ancestor's limp spirits hang from those trees
Their souls were burned as they didn't hang in effigy
Why do we ask for reparations owed us?
What country would allow such mistrust?

Our platform remains stuck in neutral
These last few years we're driving backwards
Just where Jim Crow wants us, all of us
To him supremacy means he's supreme
With the lexicon of "Domestic Terrorist"
That term has always brewed for centuries

The new "Confederacy" is composed of professionals
More sophisticated in their racism, bigotry, prejudice
They infiltrated the government that is supposed to
Protect us so that word lost its meaning and purpose
How do we defend this without trying to demean?
The fabric of the country is tearing at the seams

Stop voting against your own self interest
In fact, you must exercise your right to vote
A weaken democracy will offer little hope

Freedom's Freedom

FREEDOM'S FREEDOM 4

Belief or disbelief only one road to travel
Acceptance or un-acceptance only one-word maters
There's no third option or playing both sides
Against the middle, now you're agents of
Chaos, confusion, craziness with terror
Where is the *United States of America?*

They have been turned into war zones
By the politics that are supposed to be
For the people by the people, *what people?*

History repeats itself as historians sent out
Warnings but sheep didn't listen to anyone until
That wolf bites them the first time which is the kill shot
We are witnessing the self-destruction of this democracy
Based on lies from liars masquerading as human beings
Where are the citizens of the *United States of America?*

Who do you save? Your family, your friends,
Anyone as these oceans of discontent
Based on race or creed that religion destroy any
Seashore of hope within our future we will pay bills
You can't rob Peter to pay Paul as there's nothing left
Where are the leaders of the *United States of America?*

Quit saying we are better than this obviously we're not
Someone will rewrite history lying to say they forgot
Simple minds seek solutions to connect the dots

Freedom's Freedom

FREEDOM'S FREEDOM 5

A road less traveled means we been on it to many times
My ancestors had to go underground if they wanted
Freedom
That definition: The condition of being free
        Political independence
        Facility as of motion
        Unrestricted use of access

Has any of this applied in the last 400 years?
We're hunted, beaten, executed, and lynched
We should know our place, we could be more useful
All the gains with all the trials we're still just a commodity
We're convenient when we entertain the masses
Dunk a basketball, clown on stage or perform on the street

It's all laughs until the unspeakable truths belch
They vomit the ugliest poisoning of Humanity
This inflammation of damage seems insidious
The inflammatory lies stoke Demons of hate
Words do not matter anymore only fear
A disease such as ignorance feeds on that fear

What can some political leaders or preachers tell you?
Teach yourself to be a better version of yourself
Those rivers of filthy water flow into a
Ocean of indifference swims towards hope
That Lighthouse of dreams, passion and caring
How much better would every soul be being cleansed?

Roads and rivers more forward
Lies and schemes incite backward
It's up to you to run toward tomorrow

Freedom's Freedom

FREEDOM'S FREEDOM 6

America's mirror is stained with ugly truths
A minority in this country hands are battered
Their feet are swollen, weary as their psyche beaten
their souls washed away without jumping
None of us know what America is or will become
What will any future inherit is an interpretation?

Those scars will not heal as they burn with hate
Those tears continue to try to cleanse our pain
Those trees could ever speak of those crimes
Those voices scream for equality, emancipation
Those days my ancestors survived that lying horror
Those nights they ran towards hope dying in honor

As those elected to serve perpetuate lies
Melted with the stench of being ignorant
That definition: without education or knowledge
exhibiting a lack of education
unaware or uninformed
This invasion slaps our country backwards

We try to turn the page as the story is the same
We never get a chance to write our version of our story
We protest peacefully but we're considered looters
We cry silently for our ancestor's legacy, memory
We will fight for a better equation, situation and mercy
We know our color lines but know what we can't cross

The centuries breathe the same hallow haste
Our animosity has nothing to do with this country's shame
Liberation will come as we wipe out this racist facade

Freedom's Freedom

FREEDOM'S FREEDOM 7

What did my Great Grandfather had to endure?
What did my Grandfather's mind had to procure?
What did my Father's dreams tried to secure?
What will I have to do to prevent more misuse?
What will my son have to do to prevent abuse?
What will my future Grandson have to do to event a cure?

This is America we can't believe in
that country which condones endless new sin
environment so toxic no one wins

I'm the best version of myself to appease
I represent my Great Grandfather's distant screams
I represent my Grandfather's brilliant dreams
I represent my Father's Demons positive schemes
I represent what my son is as I will not demean
I represent what my future Grandson will be

Some of my ancestors jumped off those slave ships
None of the parameters will allow me to slip
Being an American Black man is a tough trip

Freedom's Freedom

FREEDOM'S FREEDOM 8

My future Granddaughter will be the brilliance of the future
My Daughter will have the chance to promote blessings to nurture
My Wife's love has been the foundation to provide closure

My Mother was that light without rushing comments
My Grandmothers were destined for great commitments
My Great Grandmother refused to be a prisoner of moments

Dark skies still let in a different sunlight
Clean nights shelter the rays coming in moonlight
These women are beacons monitoring what's right

Do they need hope, love, dreams, to survive those schemes?
They had to overcome systems that demean
What they did is not as easy as it seems

My story couldn't be told without their essence
Strong independence will erase any wrong dependence
All of us benefit forward so please take notice

As we try to bury all the injustice, pain, sorrow
My ancestor's strength will not forfeit or stand down or borrow
They wrote legacies in Bibles for their tomorrow

Freedom's Freedom

FREEDOM'S FREEDOM 9

The sun can come out in the morning if it wants to
On the unjust and corrupt also the true believers of tomorrow
There's no truth in this version of their America
A sad prostitution of lies, schemes, mistrust
This unyielding spit of nonfactual nonsense
Where will this vomit spew next?

The moonlight isn't allowed to erase dreams
My ancestors dreamt of their future generations
Shackled and beaten and raped by the oppressor
Physical perseverance overcame the oppression
Spiritual distance made the nights clearer
Emotional deliverance brought me here for them

If we keep saying we are better than this
Where is the identifying source of better?
We allow this prostitution to squat forward
Selling empty souls into Domestic Terror
Bringing the third world into the first order
Do you understand those psyche now America?

My ancestors followed the North Star
Where's any star of hope today?
We create them by rinsing our minds
They want us to fold in failure in every way
They open more strip clubs of discontent
Will you let it reign or move into the future America?

No more Hallelujah, Amen or Ol Lord
Educate yourself before syllables belch out
Chances are made not stolen or pimped

Freedom's Freedom

Freedom's Freedom 10

I watch every morning as I drive by those tents
I listen to the cries of chaos, piss or repent
Homelessness
This word is used in the same vein of profanity
No one says it or no one wants it
No one cares to help and no one gives a damn

I turn away when one decides the sidewalk is a toilet
offering no rinse
I cannot comprehend the understanding
Officials who continuously lie about that
Where's the funding that can stop this menace?
Where's the reform that will prevent this Hell?
Where's the empathy to think of others?

No Messiah will come for their merciless souls
They can't save themselves, we can't either
Their lives have been a pandemic as they rot as a human disease
Widespread over this entire society
cause and effect are senseless lies no one protects
Those solutions will continue to be suspect

The trash washes over the neighborhood
Their seashore eroded with chemicals
to dull this range of indifferent pain
We try to help but our voices are silenced by red tape,
white fear and blue noise
Why not offer an equal opportunity? no color lines
Why not offer some serious counseling? mental crimes
Why not offer to throw away their dreams? selfish times

Their situation is pathetic
When do these Politicians stop scheming and cheating?
How is this the Greatest Country on Earth?

TRIBUTES & PLEAS

FREEDOM BONUS 1

Another shooting of another Black Man
He's African American so you don't understand
How does a knife cut a bullet?
No one knows the situation
No one knows the media
No one knows the saturation

Our life is limited by chances
If we can just forgive glances
Diversity doesn't need romance
Sick of thoughts and prayers
Promises you never had we're better than this fad
Jim Crow said you better be glad

What you gave to how we behave
They're not going to save
Now you're in a grave

A decimated dream of different visions
Looking from a new America of equality
That broken spirit cripple's humanity
I'm tired of death
I'm tired of regrets
I'm tired of being a suspect
I'm crushed with no hope yet

Freedom never cries when you're praying
Our ancestors were begging and watching for your soul
No goals or control so Heaven and Hell knows

Freedom always lies when they're praying
Our ancestors are hoping and asking for your soul
Have a goal you can control as I don't you know

Freedom
No

FREEDOM BONUS 2

I'm desired as you're desired
I'm conscious as you're unconscious
I love to create everyday
You hate to work anyway

What happened to me?
What happened to you?
My conflict is drama
You're conflict with drama

I can't be the worst of me
You can be the worst of you
I will be the best of me
You will not be the best of you

Some story will drive me
No story will move you
I'm on Straight & Narrow Boulevard
You're on Broadway so turn left hard

I'm an institution lies for truth
you're an institution that cries for fools
Prose is my destiny
Poetry isn't your mystery

Can someone describe me?
No one can describe you
Don't stop me from writing or my pen will bleed
Don't stop you from scheming for what you need

I'm a character in my own play to my fullest life
Other characters will dismiss your sad sacrifice
This pen, pages and rage now consumes me
I hope you with the others can now see me

Experience, wisdom with schooling classed me up
Ignorance, nonsense with tragedy burned you up
My emancipation is almost complete
I just need you to cooperate when I speak

To all that know me Peace & Faith
Your love, patience and kindness equate Freedom

FREEDOM RESEARCH

Inside meant punishment
As Momma meant it
I angrily fired myself on the couch
The TV blared, it was ready to announce
Why was I going to give that a thought?
My siblings, friends and neighborhood were out
I settled in as suddenly a Black Woman stepped out

She was tall, regal with a command of language
For some strange reason my young mind was fascinated
She spoke my mind had a question which answered
Did she just say she was going to run for President?
My Momma said she was from Brooklyn in New York City
I only heard of the city by the comic books I was reading
She was surrounded as Caucasian men who listened distinctly

My memory recalls 1/25/1972
A defiant eight-year-old I do too
That punishment was a misnomer
It established a sense of order
America watched Congresswoman Shirley Chisolm
Her bravery shed our light opening that dark door
As Vice President Kamala Harris can walk in

Freedom

FREEDOM SISTERS

Raindrops of indifference intent on cleansing my soul
with an awakening of spirits defining all our goals

I thought about both my Grandmothers
my Mother, my Mom, my Godmother
my Wife, my Sisters, all Sisters
my Daughter, my Grandmother's Grandmother

My ancestors were stolen by ship from the light of Africa
my Grandmothers were born in the South in lynching Louisiana
my wife was born in the North in Philadelphia
my daughter's hope was nurtured in California

Their umber skin undaunted, their resilience, their sacrifice
those oppressors, their violations without defiance
their survival against surviving raping nights
their arrival with all the dark morning light

My Grandmother's hands beaten by thievery
clasping them in prayer to withstand tragedy
as faith put their minds at peace with confidence
as trust fueled their heart's spirit with assurance

My Daughter placing her hands on a Law Degree
my Mother walking us to school so she could see
all the pioneers demanding equality with a countless count
they sat, spoke, endured to expose the truth so we wouldn't lose count

This sunshine's substance pierces through burnt storm clouds
the rays hit all of us as we scream for now
I see my Grandmother on her porch snapping beans
I can imagine her thoughts, process, ways, means

For once the door has now opened for an umber Sister
the oppressor can't close it, the Voices have spoken

Freedom

FREEDOM'S PLEA 1

The rivers of injustice flow as raw sewage in my mind
There's no pulse or consciousness to continue to play rewind
No pathway to peace
No alley for hope

My ancestor's artifacts are never mentioned
Now their history leaves as a legacy is called into question
All roads are undone
Not a sightline for the sun

Struggles are muddy as filthy water you're drinking
Threats stinging with lies for sad, useless sheep not thinking
More room to reason
More terror in season

Elected frauds who care less for the country's welfare?
Hospitals married morgues as the dead can only stare
Sky is blue
Time is true

Freedom's Plea

Freedom's Plea 2

Why the harm in deduction as it falls back towards people of color?
When was America the land forward for others?
Nothing is sovereign
Something is rotten

Every step of land was stolen as they killed, pillaged and raped
Every landmark built with hands on backs of ancestors enslaved
Anything goes
For hurt souls

There is no such concept called peace with induction
There is an acid of hate with no reduction
Cries of democracy
Lies of false destiny

As all the stealing, cheating, killing continues as truth
As all the embers of charred bodied with gunshots
Land of opportunity
America is a tragedy

Freedom's Plea

FREEDOM'S PLEA 3

How come no soulless soul is charged when they kill?
Our youth are executed as their birth never existed
We are worthless
Justice is useless

It stands to figure our children did something wrong
They didn't get the decency of being a victim of crime
Killed for a bag of candy
Killed for a bottle of juice

Our adults are exterminated, lynched, choked, beaten
The color of authority is always whitewashed clean
Killed by brute force
Killed for no recourse

Now the only fame in this infamous society is:
A documentary
A mural or memorial
A movement

Freedom's Plea

FREEDOM'S PLEA 4

Blustery bigotry
Which winds never left the Confederacy
Now the blasts blow every direction
Their throats yelling hypocrisy with every breath

Indelible ignorance
The lives lost for skin color, misery
Insensitive rhetoric back loaded with unspeakable lies
A breaking point already broken

Condescending cowards
Sending charged up wolves off to war
Attacking the very principles of this country
Measuring senseless division one death at a time

Energized emancipation
Our ancestors are counting on us
To walk, talk or act untied as their souls do
These shackled chains of hope lift as their spirits rise

Freedom's Plea

FREEDOM'S PLEA 5

My heart beats in anger at the ogre of oppression
None of us will stop these protests with some new confession
Keep threatening me
Keep antagonizing peace

My mind is a watershed rained in piss with dirty water
This commodity of ignorance is not worth a quarter
Beating truth free
Beating dreams clean

Those elected to enact democracy are a catastrophe
Who ask this Jim Crow to put that hood back on reactionary?
You reap what you sow
That's how sad stories go

The term pandemic is not the answer to what this is
Demons are often created by old greed, mistrust or sins
The World is a Ghetto
More Pen 2 Page Rage flows

Freedom's Plea

FREEDOM'S PLEA 6

What hand will you hold tightly?
Racism/ displayed
Supremacy/ conveyed
Democracy/ delayed

What cause will you fight for?
All Lives Matter to a reaction
Equality for All with compassion
Wealth at all Cost is a distraction

Who do you believe in?
Us for the mystery
Them for the recovery
You for the discovery

I document prose in my environment
Freedom's loud voice lets me represent
The positive or negative cause and effect
America is straddling both sides of the fence

Freedom's Plea

Challenge Accepted

SEE ME

SEE ME 1

My Freedom is murdered with every negative breath I take
I can't comprehend the magnitude of this overlying truth
I can't witness anymore intellectual destruction
Which life matters? It will not be important
My life is fiction
My hope is nonfiction

Your freedom is being negotiated at all cost
There is no reform, there's no room to conform
We're being sold off in different auction blocks
It's too late to jump in the ocean of tolerance
Your life is in vain
Your hope is a game

Their Freedom is always nurtured, selfless
Every in just action counteracts a positive reaction
They never suffer at the hands of Law Enforcement
They never get an unfair trial or confinement
Their life is an illusion
Their hope has a conclusion

When will any America stand for mercy?
Who is responsible for this injustice, mistrust?
How will this narrative erase us?

Freedom isn't free

See Me 2

The temperature of ignorance has melted this America's boiling plate
Nothing is delicate now; every word slaps you in the mouth
Every soul is weary of the mismanagement of Democracy
Color is equated to race that equals division
Multiply the hate
Add more debate

In an age of media that is social, no thought is safe
If you push that send button the scrutiny is up for discussion
There's no capitol in capitalism just petty corruption of thieves
We eat it as if it was breakfast cereal for mass consumption
Divide and conquer
Subtract with horror

There's no perfection in belief only malice
Only crisis into many receipts as bills are due
Our minds won't tune out more debris now its trash
Options are optics with no debrief or asylum
Overblown lies offer no relief or stimulus checks
This is the chaos that's well received

Will they lie stating their intentions are misconstrued?
Who will say over and over their words are misused?
How are those reparations with no issues to include?

Freedom isn't free

SEE ME 3

This gospel of ignorance continues to be preached
These aimless sheep death in imminent
Sounds of fraud sing a vaulted melody
My lungs fill with poisonous anger built on aggression
Fists balled up
Mind coiled up

We have been beaten, brutalized, burned
they will haunt, harass, hunt, hypnotize
We will become better, bolder, brazen
They have been scared, senseless and sullen
Memorialize hope
Mobilize healing

The moist skies must shine sunlight untied
A mist of pretense washes over Democracy
A rain of salvation dries with discovery
My ancestor's souls are swollen seeking validation
Cries aren't suspicious
Lies are malicious

When will you evict the Oppressor from your mind?
Why would you let the whispers steal your time?
How does this situation bury us?

Freedom isn't free

SEE ME 4

My mind, body, soul will not be crippled by their fear
My ancestor's psyche sacrifice is abundantly clear
My reluctance to document will not offer a tear
My hope is that more moments of prose will have a peer
Writing is understanding
Reading is misunderstanding

This unjust mental contraband box me in the wrong corner
The neighborhood's punch comes out swinging as it's never over
Most of the Zombies are lost with a disorder
In a search for truth there are no burnt boarders
Seeing believes
Hearing is achieving

The definition of Freedom is not just for the free
My ancestor's plight, struggles and pain always define me
We are still facing the same hardships you see
Don't ask me that perplexed question, how can this be?
Tasting dirty dreams
Touching clean screams

When will the terror stop being reality?
Who will take the baton of destiny?
How will hope to save us?

Freedom isn't free

SEE ME 5

Only time will stop your accomplishments
Only confidence will build your acceptance
Only strength will honor your achievements
Only fear will cause anymore arguments
Failure breeds success
Truth can confess

As the life gets choked out of us
Compassion was stabbed by ignorance
Decisions keep vomiting mass destruction
Attrition's violence erodes every America
Pain is in my eyes
Fame doesn't cry

Obligation is self-awareness towards faith
The discipline is not swallowed by anarchy
400 years of oppression didn't stop our Humanity
Now these adverse adjectives swim in my soul
Displaced as delusional or dishonored
Where do we go? Where are my goals?

Misery slept with nothing
Healing amounts to something
Hope ask for anything

Freedom isn't free

SEE ME 6

My eyes are tired of seeing all this destruction
My heart is tired of tasting more bad decisions
My feet are tired of running in clean darkness
My ears is tired of listening to wrong desires
Those goals disappear
Those souls defend

I think this Country's madness will never stop
I know what 400 years of oppression is about
I wish that skin color wouldn't give the news clout
I say that we all have fears without a doubt
Their dreams are nightmares
Their schemes are everywhere

They continue to push poison propaganda
They continue to not allow for Miranda
They continue to misuse the justice system
They continue to privatize filling prisons
Should you educate?
Would you escalate?

Why are you satisfied with nothing?
When are you going to fight for something?
How are you falling for anything?

Freedom isn't free

www.vagabondbooks.net